A TRIBUTE TO MY MOTHER

A TRIBUTE TO MY MOTHER

Reflections on Life, Love, and Loss

Sophia Blankson

ReadersMagnet, LLC

A Tribute to My Mother: Reflections on life, love, and loss
Copyright © 2019 by Sophia Blankson. All rights reserved.

Published in the United States of America
ISBN Paperback: 978-1-949981-32-2
ISBN eBook: 978-1-948864-99-2

All rights reserved. No part of this publication may be reproduced, stored in a retrieval system or transmitted in any way by any means, electronic, mechanical, photocopy, recording or otherwise without the prior permission of the author except as provided by USA copyright law.

The opinions expressed by the author are not necessarily those of ReadersMagnet, LLC.

ReadersMagnet, LLC
10620 Treena Street, Suite 230 | San Diego, California, 92131 USA
1.619. 354. 2643 | www.readersmagnet.com

Book design copyright © 2019 by ReadersMagnet, LLC. All rights reserved.
Cover design by Sophia Blankson & Ericka Walker
Interior design by Shemaryl Evans
Interior images by Sophia Blankson

Acknowledgements

MY SINCERE THANKS GO to Mr. Paul Aidoo who was gracious enough to review and edit my poems. I truly appreciate all the wise suggestions he gave.

Special thanks go to Peggy J. Ballard, my art instructor, who encouraged me to include some of my art work in this book. When I wasn't sure I could do it, she believed in me and helped me along the way.

Thanks to Bill Nord, whose creative work with the camera, produced the author's picture.

I also thank Steevan Sicklesteel, our computer guru, who massaged the pictures and made them fit the format needed for the first edition.

Last but by no means the least, my fathomless thanks to my husband, Dr. Charles C. Blankson, who provided all the support I needed to finish this book.

Dedication

THIS BOOK IS DEDICATED to my mother, Joana Baisie, also known affectionately as Memaa. She was born on May 26, 1925 in Cape Coast, Ghana and passed away in Accra on May 24, 1995.

My mother had a beautiful voice and would sing to us or to herself as she went about her daily chores. The singing stopped. Instead, she built a cold wall of silence around her when life became rough on her.

To her mother, my grandmother and great grandmother, all of whom were blessed with long life, and who lived to share their singing and some fun time with us.

To the many "mothers" that I have had in my new life in America. I felt all your love and embrace as I sought to find meaning in my new home, here in America.

To all mothers and grandmothers who sacrifice so much for their children and grandchildren, often to the extent of neglecting their own wellbeing and shelving their own dreams.

And to my husband, Charles "I love you." My children Ekua, Araba and Koby who made it all worthwhile during the rough times. I pray that God would help me keep singing to you.

Introduction

$\mathcal{A}$S MUCH AS MANY have proudly embraced the United States of America as their home, many naturalized Americans live torn lives having given up one form of living to accept what America offers. One hardly can let go of the life, the family and friends left behind in search of a better life.

They say "blood is thicker than water", and that is very true. The vast land or oceans that might separate you and your family will never dilute the thickness of the blood you share with your parents and siblings. Time may ease the pain, you may seek or be taken in by American families. The pain will linger on as long as you know they are not getting enough to eat or have the same privileges as you do.

You try to share what you have by providing for your parents as well as providing for other family members. The pain intensifies when others take advantage of your generosity. The parents are those who hurt the most when they are denied what is due them. In some cases they can't read your new language, so when they receive letters from you, they need help from others to read and translate to them. You live in two worlds, the one you left behind in pursuit of a better life, and the one that can't fully accept you because of your color or how you sound.

From time to time, little things of your new life will suddenly transport you to your old life. Life, as we know it is the same in the east or the west, the north or south. We all breathe air and need water to quench our thirst. We all lie down to sleep, be it on a feathered bed or straw mat. Sleep may even come quicker to the one sleeping on the mat than those on satin-draped and fitted feathered bed.

The other issue dealt with in the poem is sadness brought to children from those they love most. When parents make wrong choices, the pain may stay with the children, not only the little children, but the offspring of two people who used to love each other, at whatever age they may be. The adults may settle their differences and move on, but invariably, the children may never know the true meaning behind the chaos and pretence.

Seeing your mother change from the happy, beautiful person to an unhappy and morose person was difficult for a teenager to bear. Then I grew up, married and had my own family. Life was good, but we had to give it up to come to America, thinking it would be for a short time. Circumstances changed back home and we changed so we didn't go back. I had to deal with some ups and downs. Life is but give and take. I read and learned from all that I could lay my hands on. I listened to how others have come through life and found good role models. All of a sudden you start to see some of the mistakes of your parents and being so far away, there is very little that you can do. You try to put meaning to what you witnessed as a child and make yourself even more helpless. The brain is such a powerful tool, storing the good and the bad memories, having very little control on what will trigger and bring out buried feelings.

It was at one of such times that having heard a hymn that my mother used to sing that a whole stream of feeling came to me. I sat down and wrote about 14 verses. At the next opportunity, I sent two copies to relatives and asked them to read it to my mom. They didn't. Less than a year later, she got sick and died.

I was able to go to the funeral. Six verses were printed in the funeral brochure as a tribute at the funeral. There was a glitch during the printing. Consequently the brochures could not be delivered in time for the funeral service. At a later date in the United States, I was able to finally have others hear it at a memorial service that we held for her. You know we live in two worlds, hence even mourning your dead must be in duplicates.

Over the years, I have added and taken some verses away in an attempt to publish my poetry. This past May was my mother's twenty-third anniversary. The time went by so fast especially when it means I am twenty three years older. Time shouldn't go too fast. We have to savor life. I finally decided this poetry should stand by itself. To do that, I had to complete the story I started writing years ago.

This is a story about life and the disappointments it might bring. There is always hope and victory ahead if you look to a higher source.

I hope that by releasing this current edition, some mother or father whose eyes have been dimmed with tears of regret, poor health, dashed dreams will wipe the tears away and see how precious life can be. I say to you, "Don't give up. Life has its curves and turns. Joy may be a curve away, so keep on going and looking for the gold at the end of the rainbow." Keep on singing, dreaming, or what ever you like to do.

A Tribute To My Mother

I heard a song you used to sing

And remembered your voice, so sweet and calm

But you stopped to sing

For life was too rough and hard to claim.

I remember your face and smile

So sweet and full of joy

But you stopped to smile

For life was too painful and void of joy.

I remember the way you used to talk

So soft to humbly guide us through our day.

But you stopped to care nor talk

For you rather wore a frown in a way.

I remember all the little things we shared.

The good and the bad things in life.

But you thought you were the only one wronged.

And there was no one to show you a better life.

I remember some of the rough times.

They come to us to draw us closer to God.

But you stopped to pray for your pains.

For you were also led away from God.

I remember the tears you used to shed.

It was difficult to know why you had to cry.

But I guess it helped to build a wall

From those who wanted to help or pry.

I remember your many travels.

You didn't know where you belong.

But you did your best in your searching

For you will come back to us before too long,

I remember one man called Jesus.

He died on a cross to save you and me.

When you turn to Him in prayers

Your life He'll turn around and save.

I remember the good times He has brought me.

And He is so close to help in the rough times.

His joy I cannot fully tell about

For you must experience it at the right time.

I ask myself, will I hear you sing again?

The answer is yes, if to Jesus you will come.

There'll be a place for you in His heavenly choir.

For you to sing in joy for all the world again.

I ask myself, will I see her smile again?

The answer is yes, if the frown you'll wipe away.

God will put a smile in your heart again.

To warm your soul and the smile you will attain.

I ask myself, does she know what's her deed?

Five lovely souls and more you have planted

In God's garden to serve and love in need.

To toil and tend all those who care to ask.

So know today that you are loved indeed.

By God and His Son and all of us.

Open your heart to His calling when in need.

To experience His love and the love from us.

Let go of the hard and miserable times.

Wipe away the tears of pain.

God will turn your hurt into joyful tunes

For all to hear and cherish again.

Don't let these last days be wasted.

Seek the face of God and receive His peace.

Let His love shine through till it has lasted.

He has a path in His family plan for you to trace.

I wonder if these words ever got to your ears.

So humbly written to be shared with you.

I had to pass them through people I thought cared,

But oh, how they changed and had no care for you.

I prayed and prayed that your pain may ease.

The full story I never got to know.

But I prayed the more for a release,

Hoping our God finds a way to help now.

It wasn't too long in months when the phone rang.

Those late night or early morning calls

Send a chilling blood through your spine at the ring.

Still hoping the reason warrants such calls.

The news was that you were sick.

Very, very sick and had to be admitted.

The helplessness, not knowing all makes one sick.

All you can do is pray and be agitated.

Wanting to know what is going on was not easy.

Very little was said, may be to spare you the pain.

Things are done differently there, nothing comes easy.

All you can do is pray and hope that it will not be in vain.

The wait was long, each day dragging by.

The news was not forthcoming.

Things were looking better as the days went by.

What a relief, good things are happening.

But the joy would not last that long.

All the planning on your part to make things better,

Would have to curtail before long.

Things have changed, the planning will not matter.

The big news finally came in one early morning.

The numbness that followed the chill.

The helplessness, that comes with mourning.

The sweet small voice was now stilled.

I remember the gripping pain of sorrow.

Death is inevitable, that's what they say.

Even when you know it may come today or tomorrow,

You can never be prepared for the frightful day.

You know you should be strong for all.

You are the one who is optimistic that all will be well.

But the pain of death drains the strength out of you.

And leaves you helpless and unwell.

Then comes the time of blaming and finger-pointing.

You reason and battle over what went wrong.

Till finally you realize that all the pining

Will never right the wrong.

In the sadness of that day,

I heard the song you used to sing.

Is it to tell me the final ray

Is going on to be with the King?

Oh, that dreadful spring day.

When new life should be beaming,

Becomes the final way

That your light was dying.

The planning, the preparation

Was not easy forthcoming.

When there is such a distance of separation,

Makes things not easy going.

However hard and long the planning,

It seemed it will never be completed.

The list kept getting longer and ongoing,

For everything must be obtained.

Then came the time to go and say farewell.

The journey took several hours to make.

My first time after leaving those I loved so well.

How much would I be able to take?

Things had changed and I have changed.

What made sense to me then didn't anymore.

If only the reason of the journey could be changed

Then some of the changes I could adore.

The obstacles were many.

Man-made and nature taking its course.

But there was help in bounty.

And everything seemed to find its course.

It was a Thursday night we kept the wake.

Many came to sing their farewells.

The air was solemn, their peace they made.

Till morning lights ushered in the bells.

We journeyed to your home town.

For that was where you would rest in peace.

The eldest of the brood had flown

And her place would forever be a space.

The service, the farewells, too hard to bear.

The singing, the pacing cannot calm the pain.

But all was done, the end was near.

What had to be done nothing could refrain.

The end had come, we've sent you off.

We did our best, the best we could.

The time had come, you are on your own,

Never again to see you, until in God's world.

Your absence had been difficult to bear.

The many roles you filled none can take.

You shouldn't have stopped singing dear.

For now all we remember is the frown.

Time had ran by so fast.

Not all had been well.

But all too soon time had passed

And there's not a lot to dwell.

Twenty-three years have come and gone,

Some good times that you've missed.

But the bad we are glad you were gone.

The pain you had been spared.

All we can do is hope and pray.

You made your peace while here below.

And now all you do is watch and be gay?

For those you loved to care and follow.

A little note for you who read

Don't forget to sing the songs you love.

Many will remember the songs when you are gone.

The voice that brought them love.

Don't forget to wear a smile.

It takes less effort to smile than frown.

Think of what would bring a smile,

And on your face it will be drawn.

Sow seeds of love all around you,

They'll bear good fruits when you're gone.

Your good works will follow you,

And now my story is done.

The End!

www.ingramcontent.com/pod-product-compliance
Lightning Source LLC
LaVergne TN
LVHW020739090526
838202LV00057BA/5989